ANSELM BOOKS

Should a Christian support guerillas?

Richard Harries

Dean, King's College London

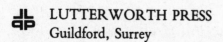

LUTTERWORTH PRESS
Guildford, Surrey

I am grateful to Professor Gordon Dunstan of King's College, London, who originally guided me to explore the Just War/ Just Revolution tradition; to those whose comments in response to lectures and articles over the years have helped me develop the argument set out in the book; to Jean Holm and The Very Reverend Peter Baelz for their detailed comments on the draft manuscript and to Evelyn Wimbush for her typing.

Richard Harries

By the same author
Prayers of Grief and Glory *(Lutterworth Press)*
Being a Christian *(Mowbrays)*

First published 1982

ISBN 0-7188-2517-9

Set in 11/12pt. Bembo
Printed in Great Britain by Lonsdale Universal Printing Ltd., Bath, Avon.

Contents

The editors say . . .

Anselm Books are written specially for lay people who want to think about their faith. They will help explore important matters of Christian belief and action.

Each book deals with a single question—about God, or Jesus Christ, or the Church, or the Bible, or prayer, or bringing up children in the faith, or marriage, or abortion, or euthanasia, or the use of nuclear power . . .

Why *Anselm?* Anselm was a great Christian scholar of the eleventh century who became Archbishop of Canterbury. The original title in English of one of his best known books was *Faith Seeking Understanding.*

Peter Baelz
Dean of Durham Cathedral

Jean Holm
Lecturer in Charge of Religious Studies,
Homerton College, Cambridge

1
Are non-revolutionaries living in mortal sin?

Camillo Torres—the man of 'headlong straightness'
Camillo Torres was the son of a well-off doctor. He was brought up in a comfortable and apparently loving home. (After Camillo's death his mother wrote a moving defence of his actions to the Pope.) At university, unsure of what career to follow, he went on vacation to a place where he could be on his own. 'I realised that life as I understood it, as I was living it, lacked meaning. I thought I could be more useful socially.' He then analysed the professions one by one, medicine, law, engineering . . . he thought of God. 'It seemed to me a total solution. The most logical. I returned to Bogota determined to enter the monastery of the Dominicans.'

Camillo Torres qualified as a sociologist, as well as a priest, and in due course he became a lecturer at Colombia University. Over the years he had gradually become more socially aware and politically active. At Colombia University he helped found a political party and eventually lost his job for the part he played in some student demonstrations. As the pressure on his party increased and as the chance of achieving social reforms by peaceful means seemed to diminish, he took to the mountains and joined a guerilla band. He was killed in 1966 in a skirmish with government forces.

In *The Observer* of 28th October, 1979, there was an article on the child coal miners of Colombia. Boys of under 12, who work nine hours a day in un-propped galleries that can collapse at any moment, earn 10p a sack. The Colombian

Government closes its eyes to this child slavery to avoid trouble with the mine owners. So things still have not changed much.

Camillo Torres believed that 'the duty of every Catholic is to be a revolutionary'. Moreover he shared with Che Guevara the conviction that 'the duty of every revolutionary is to make the revolution'. In short, 'The Catholic who is not a revolutionary is living in mortal sin'.

The life of Camillo Torres forces Christians to think again about the morality of armed revolution. He may or may not have been right in what he taught and did. It is the purpose of this book to explore that question in relation to him and others who feel impelled to take the same revolutionary path. A man who started off with a simple desire 'to be more useful socially', and who was led by his experience of God and the conditions in Colombia to take up arms against the Government because he believed that revolution was, as he put it, 'the only effective and far-reaching way to make the love of all people a reality', puts a question mark against many traditional assumptions. In the words of Peter Levi, the poet and literary critic, 'there was a headlong straightness about him; it is part of his victory that no religious man today would dare to be sure that God was not closer to Camillo Torres than to most of us.'

Camillo Torres is the best know Christian revolutionary. But he is not alone. One experienced observer of the South American scene has commented, 'Nowadays a radical clergy is something one takes for granted. Most governments look nervously over their shoulders at their priests.' Camillo Torres accuses most of us of living in mortal sin. Let us see if he is right. Let us examine some of the arguments we might use to counter his accusation.

'Jesus taught pacifism'—or did he?
There are many different kinds of pacifism. Here we focus on only one, and that very briefly. It is reported that Jesus taught

'You have learned that they were told, "Love your neighbour, hate your enemy." But what I tell you is this: Love your enemies and pray for your persecutors' (Matt. 5: 43). All practising Christians have a duty to obey this teaching, and it is difficult to see how loving one's enemy is compatible with taking up arms against him with the strong possibility that this will lead to his death or injury. But at the same time as loving our enemy we are bound to love our family, our friends, and all those to whom we are bound by loyalty or compassion.

In the north east of Brazil the rural population is 70 per cent illiterate, mostly unemployed and in debt to the company stores. The urban population is 60 per cent illiterate, underemployed or unemployed and rootless. A farming and sugar plantation oligarchy owns almost all the land and its members are fiercely opposed to change. The average annual per capita income is about £60 per year. The infant mortality rate is 60 per cent and the average life expectancy is about 35 years. A Christian living in north east Brazil is in duty bound to remember Jesus's saying that he has to love the wealthy oligarchy whose insensitivity or inertia is responsible for all this suffering. But is is hardly surprising if he is first of all filled with a burning love for those round him who are suffering and dying daily.

So the command to love our enemy cannot be considered in isolation from love of those who are the victims of our enemy. Furthermore, in what does love of the enemy consist?

In one of his letters (to Marcellinus) Augustine commented on the teaching of Jesus in the Sermon on the Mount. He argued that if you take away freedom from an aggressor you are in fact doing him good. For nothing could be worse, suggested Augustine, than letting him be successful, for then evil is strengthened both in the world and within the aggressor himself. So, not only do we have to balance love of the enemy with love of those being hurt by the enemy, but

3

we have to ask what it actually means to love our enemy. Does not loving an enemy mean bringing home to him the harm he is doing, by stopping him inflicting suffering on others?

It could be argued, however, that the command to love our enemy is only a general principle and that Jesus made it quite clear what this involved in another saying, 'You have learned that they were told, "Eye for eye, tooth for tooth." But what I tell you is this: Do not set yourself against the man who wrongs you. If someone slaps you on the right cheek, turn and offer him your left. If a man wants to sue you for your shirt, let him have your coat as well. If a man in authority makes you go one mile, go with him two' (Matt. 5: 38 – 41).

If we examine this text we note that the first example of a wrong done to us is an insult rather than an injury. It is the right cheek that is struck, i.e., it has been hit with the back of the right hand and this was generally accepted as a way of insulting someone. The second illustration refers to a legal situation. The third probably refers to being pressed into service by one of the Roman authorities. Of these examples, then, it is clear that only the third is at all applicable to the question of whether it is right or wrong to take up arms against a person who oppresses us. And is even that decisive?

Two points about these three examples can be noted. First, none of them deals with a situation where serious injury is being inflicted. Second, none of them indicates what you are to do if it is other people who are suffering terribly. They all refer to *you*. They do not say what you are to do if your children are being attacked.

It is obvious to anyone who reads the New Testament that Jesus was not a legalist, that is, he did not lay down detailed rules about how we are to behave in any and every situation. In a story by P. G. Wodehouse, Battling Bilson offers the other cheek and then when that is hit punches the other person on the jaw on the grounds that 'A man has only two cheeks'! Jesus taught us that we are to love one another, and then gave some vivid illustrations of what this might involve. The saying about not setting ourself against someone who wrongs us needs to be taken with the utmost seriousness, but did Jesus really mean to rule out, for all time, protection of the weak from those who are causing them to suffer? If this really was his intention surely he would have given illustrations which referred to *serious injury,* and serious injury done, say, to *defenceless children* rather than to those he was addressing, most of who would have been men? The words of the great seventeenth century founder of International Law, Hugo Grotius, remain applicable,

> If the right of . . . defending the citizens by arms against robbers and plunderers, was taken away, then would follow a vast licence of crime and a deluge of evils; since even now, while criminal judgments are administered, violence is hardly repressed. Therefore if the mind of Christ had been to induce such a state of things as never was heard of, undoubtedly He would have set it forth in the clearest and most special words, and would have commanded that none should pronounce capital sentence, none should wear arms; which we nowhere read that He did; for what is adduced to this effect is either very general or obscure.

There are many other texts that could be discussed, some of which point to the acceptance by Jesus of the possibility of a just use of armed force. The two we have looked at are the ones most often cited by pacifists in support of their case. But as the argument has tried to show these sayings are not conclusive.

Camillo Torres accused non-revolutionaires of living in mortal sin. The pacifist denies this, saying that Jesus taught pacifism. But the case is far from proved. The challenge of Torres remains.

'I fought for my country against the Nazis but I would never rebel against my own government'

This is the most widespread attitude to war and revolution amongst Christians in Europe. In England, for example, most people think it was right to fight against the Nazis, but regard it as wrong under any circumstances to take up arms against a government, even when that government is illegal and itself in a state of rebellion against the crown, as was Mr Smith's regime in Rhodesia. But will this absolute distinction hold?

1. Those Christians who take their stand firmly on the words of the Bible quote Romans 13: 1 – 2 which says, 'Every person must submit to the supreme authorities. There is no authority but by act of God, and the existing authorities are instituted by him; consequently anyone who rebels against authority is resisting a divine institution.' This text has been particularly influential in the thought of the followers of Martin Luther (1483 – 1546) and some people maintain that this influence helped create a climate of opinion in which Hitler was able to maintain power. People were conditioned to obey the state even though they often knew that the state was carrying our wicked acts.

But what about another passage which is relevant, Revelation 13: 5 – 6? This chapter describes a great beast. 'The beast was allowed to mouth bombast and blasphemy, and was given the right to reign for forty-two months. It opened its mouth in blasphemy against God, reviling his name and his heavenly dwelling.' The beast in this passage is the Roman Empire. And it is clear that the state in that condition, far from being an instrument of God, has usurped the power of God and so become demonic. It is no longer the state to which we owe lawful authority. Because it has become demonic, it no longer has any claim over us. It is no longer the state described in Romans 13.

2.   Is the state the only institution to which we owe loyalty? We have an allegiance to our church, to our ethnic group, to our political party and so on. In Europe during the fifteenth and sixteenth centuries, when the states as we know them were struggling to emerge, and when there was a strong papacy competing with rulers for the allegiance of all citizens, it was natural that people should have been taught to obey the state under all circumstances, and that no foothold for legitimate rebellion should have been allowed. The influence of that earlier teaching is still with us. But the nation-state is always, to some extent, an arbitrary thing and often it has been brought about by conquest. For some people, e.g. the Kurds, who live under a number of different states in Iran, Iraq and Turkey, allegiance to their ethnic group is stronger than their loyalty to their respective government. There seems no good reason in logic or morality to deny the validity of the stronger claim they feel.

The struggle of one group, to whom we owe allegiance, against another one, to whom we also feel a loyalty, is not so exceptional. Certainly, there can be no absolute divide between struggle against the evil of an aggressor state and struggle within that state against an aggressive government. If there was that divide, it would lead to the absurd situation that the allies were right to fight against Hitler with the might of external armies but those who tried to kill him from within Germany were wrong.

'Stand up and give 'em a few hard pokes'
So far we have argued only that Jesus did not explicitly teach pacifism, and that there is no absolute distinction between fighting for one's country against an external aggressor and fighting againt a tyrannical government. These are negative arguments. Nothing has been said to imply that Christians ought to join an armed rising.

7

To test our reactions let us begin with a simple situation in personal relationships. In a particular marriage the wife is a doormat. She meekly complies with her husband's every wish. He is not consciously cruel or bullying but he expects and gets his own way in every situation and he never considers his wife's feelings except in a somewhat patronising way. Most of us, faced with that domestic tyranny, want the wife to begin to stand up to her husband, however painful it may be for her and however disruptive to the household. We feel she owes it to her humanity to do so. Only by standing up to him will she do justice to the dignity of her existence as a human being.

What is true in a domestic situation is true in a wider context. It may be that resistance, even armed resistance, to the oppressor, is a moral imperative—what has been called, 'the last flicker of humanity'. D. H. Lawrence put this in his own inimitable way,

> Stand up, stand up for justice,
> Ye swindled little blokes!
> Stand up and do some punching,
> Give 'em a few hard pokes.

Most pacifists today would agree with the sentiment in that poem. They would stress that pacifism is not the same as passivity. They would point to the range of non-violent measures that can be taken to assert the need for jutice. To take just one example, no one would accuse the Archbishop of North Brazil, Helder Camara, of failing to stand up for the suffering poor in his diocese. His constant message is justice and it has been heard, if not responded to, by the authorities. His house has been machine gunned, his chaplain has disappeared. He has said,

Today, I am becoming one of the voiceless poor of Brazil. Only on local radio can my voice be heard. The national press and radio are forbidden to report anything I say. When I am attacked in the most

widely read newspapers, I am not allowed the use of the media to reply
. . . yet conditions are steadily getting worse. I must continue to fight for
the human rights of my people.

By fighting, Helder Camara does not mean using arms. His
methods are explicitly, avowedly non-violent. He sees
himself, unashamedly, as a character like Don Quixote. 'I am
very fond of Don Quixote. He is much more realistic than is
generally believed. When I face a crowd of people as I did
tonight, I have the impression that my talk about overthrowing structures without armed force is, for a number of
the young, quixotic. And yet there is realism in it, I might
say political realism . . .' So pacifists like Helder Camara are
entirely at one with those who say that it is morally necessary
for people to stand up for themselves and get their oppressors
off their backs. The question then becomes a matter of means.
We have already seen that violent means cannot be
definitively ruled out by the teaching of Jesus. The question is
whether there are positive reasons which might make it a
matter of obligation to use force.

'Make sure your boots are greased'
The quotations from Helder Camara reveal that for pacifists
like him the end to be achieved, greater social justice, is
important and that non-violent agitation is a means of
achieving that end. But the question is, suppose those means
do not achieve the desired end, suppose there are better or
quicker means, means which involve less suffering for fewer
people? In Zimbabwe it cannot be denied that it was the
military action of the United Front that brought about the
fall of the Smith Government. Talk, diplomacy and sanctions
by themselves failed to do this. There are important questions
about ends which have to be asked, but if the end is seen in
terms of the overthrow of the Smith Government, for
example, then does it become a *moral* matter to use the means
most likely to achieve that end? Suppose a military dictator to

be holding out in a presidential palace with machine guns and stores of ammunition. One way of overthrowing him would be for massed crowds of unarmed civilians to walk up to the palace and ask for his surrender—and if this was refused, to continue to chant. In the end, I suspect, the soldiers would lose their nerve and machine gun the crowd. Another tactic would be for an aeroplane to bomb the palace. This course of action would be more effective, quicker and less costly in terms of human life.

There is a great deal of unreality in both the politics and religion of most of us, but if we are serious about the ends we champion, a sign of that seriousness is being prepared to examine the best means to achieve those ends. If we will a particular end a sign of our sincerity is whether we will the means to achieve that end. This does not mean that every means is morally permissible. We have yet to see whether some means are absolutely ruled out, for example, indiscriminate terrorism, but the use of all force cannot, on a sober examination of the teaching of Jesus, be absolutely ruled out for Christians. Armed force is one of the means which might have to be employed. The 'might' in this sentence means more than 'could', it has moral overtones, that is, if we are serious about achieving a certain end we might *morally* have to use certain military means. If we are serious it might mean 'keeping your rifle oiled and your boots greased'.

We began with the challenge, posed by Camillo Torres, that non-revolutionary Christians are living in mortal sin. This accusation has not yet been fully answered. All we have shown so far is that people owe it to their humanity, to their dignity as persons, to stand up to those who are oppressing or in any way enslaving them. This standing up may be done by non-violent means, writing, protest marches and so on. But in certain circumstances it could be a moral matter to use force, if this was thought to be the only possible or the most humane way of achieving a desired end.

2
What can past Christians teach us?

It would be absurd to approach the ethical problem of armed revolution as though this was a new question. Christians in the past have often been forced to think about the matter and it may be that they can offer us some valuable guidelines.

The first Christian centuries

Until Christianity became the official religion of the Roman Empire at the beginning of the fourth century most Christians were pacifists. This pacifism may have had a number of motives, for example, soldiers (above a certain rank anyway) were forced to sacrifice to statues of Caesar. But, that apart, Christians were hardly likely to be found backing armed uprisings. They were, for much of this time, a tiny sect. They were subject to periodic persecution. They did not want to cause more trouble for themselves by rebellion. On the contrary, they wanted to convince the Roman world that they were good citizens, indeed the very soul of that world.

Tyrannicide

In the early middle ages the question of Tyrannicide was discussed. If a ruler became a tyrant what could be done to get rid of him? In the twelfth century a Christian philosopher known as *John of Salisbury* said that as a good ruler was in the image of God, an oppressive one was in the image of the devil and could be struck down. Sometimes God would strike him down through a natural disaster, at other times God would use a human hand. People who struck down tyrants in this way were to be regarded as 'servants of the Lord'.

Thomas Aquinas

The great Christian theologian, Thomas Aquinas (1225 – 74), drew a distinction between those who usurped a throne and those who, though they were legitimate rulers, became tyrannical in their behaviour. Those who had no legal right to rule should, Aquinas taught, be resisted wherever this was possible. Modern examples of the kind of situation he was referring to would be the military government in Chile which overthrew by force a democratically elected government, the Smith regime in Rhodesia which illegally declared its independence and the Russian puppet regime in Afghanistan.

Those who become tyrannical in their behaviour should also be resisted. But Aquinas makes three important qualifications. First, action to depose the ruler must be taken by public authority. He rejected the view that any individual could strike down a tyrant on his own initiative. Obviously what is meant by 'public authority' varies from society to society but the import is clear—the senior men in a state acting through such political institutions as there are. Second, the situation must be really extreme. If the tyranny is not utterly intolerable it may be wiser to accept it because those who take action against a tyrant often fail and this leads to greater repression. Further, the danger of setting up a new tyranny is always present, particularly if outside help is called in. Third, those who are acting must consider very carefully the consequences of their actions. In his discussion on sedition Aquinas says that overthrowing a tyrannical ruler does not count as tyranny 'except perhaps in the case that it is accompanied by such disorder that the community suffers greater harm from the consequent disturbance than it would from a continuation of the former rule'. In other words, those contemplating action have to consider very carefully the extent of civil upheaval they are going to bring about and weigh this against the ills of the tyrannic rule. Only if the former is likely to be less than the latter is it morally legitimate to act. This important piece of common sense is sometimes called the principle of proportion. It is clear, then, that Aquinas does not rule out the possibility of a just revolution, but he lays down important conditions which must be observed if it is to count as ethically right.

The tradition which accepted, with caution, the possibility in certain circumstances of such a thing as a just revolution and which began with Aquinas was consolidated in the teaching of a Spanish theologian, *Suarez* (1548 – 1617). The emphasis in Suarez on counting the cost is even more pronounced. For example, even when the ruler is one who has usurped the throne we have to consider the consequences of trying to kill him. Suarez says that if all it means is that the son of the tyrant or one of his friends takes over it is not legitimate 'because in the event of such a slaughter evil is done without hope of effecting thereby a greater good and because in such a case the state is not actually defended or freed from tyranny'. When the situation is one of a legitimate ruler acting with such cruelty over a long period of time that it becomes literally intolerable then, 'the said state, acting as a whole and in accordance with the public and general deliberations of its communities and leading men, may depose him'. But this must be done 'prudently, without causing greater injury to the people'. Suarez explicitly states that the conditions for waging a just revolution are the same as those laid down for waging a just war. These conditions apply to the period before a war and also to its conduct. These, and their application to the modern period, are considered later.

Anglican attitudes
Whereas the pre- and post-reformation Catholic tradition allowed for the possibility of a just revolution, Anglican

writers have, until the last decade, set their minds firmly against such a thing. It is understandable enough. The emergence of the nation state, and the break with Rome, made it politically necessary to concentrate all authority in the secular ruler. Anglican hostility to resistance of any kind reached its peak with the doctrine of the divine right of kings. *Lancelot Andrewes* (1555 – 1626), a famous Bishop of the Church of England, preached a sermon on the story of David and Saul, describing the incident when David had Saul in his grasp and could have killed him but chose not to. 'Saul,' said Andrewes, 'was a tyrant, a demoniac, an enemy' but nothing, nothing at all, could justify David killing Saul, for Saul was a rightful ruler. And the example, said Lancelot Andrewes, was binding on all people for all time. In so far as the Anglican Church has a distinctive moral tradition it is to be found in the teaching of the Caroline Divines—those learned and devout Anglicans who taught during the middle of the 17th century. They were extremely hostile to any kind of resistance. Jeremy Taylor, at one time Chaplain to Charles I, likened resistance to a lawful ruler to witchcraft and considered it to be the most damnable of sins. Robert Sanderson wrote, 'To take up arms offensive or defensive against a lawful sovereign cannot be done by any man, at any time, in any case, upon any colour or pretension whatsoever'.

Yet, in 1688 there came 'The Glorious Revolution'. James II, against the whole tenor of the teaching of the Church of England for two centuries, was deposed, with London clergy playing a leading role. Political necessity threw overboard the strongest teaching.

The uncompromisingly negative Anglican attitude towards resistance to lawful authority has had far reaching consequences. When men found they had to act otherwise than the doctrine dictated they had no ethical or theological basis with which to guide and justify what they did. It meant that in the eighteenth century Anglican political theology, if we can call it that, ceased to exist. People thought that religion was concerned only with what went on in the heart and mind, yet at the same time they accepted that the arrangement of English society (with its big gap between rich and poor) was ordained by God. At the end of the eighteenth century, with the fear of the French revolution, this unthinking conservatism became vociferous and bishops in the House of Lords fiercely denounced the whole idea of revolution.

The Lutheran tradition

Martin Luther, who sparked off the Reformation in the six-teenth century, taught that God ruled all aspects of human life but that he did so in two different ways. He ruled secular life, in particular the state, through force, but he ruled the Christian fellowship through the persuasive power of love alone. All Christians are subject to both forms of God's rule. A Christian is a citizen, a member of the state, and must pay attention to the teaching in Romans 13 about obedience to the state.

When the peasants revolted in 1524 – 25 Luther wrote a strong letter to them condemning what they were doing. 'Suffering! Suffering! Cross! Cross! This and nothing else is the Christian law,' he wrote to them. Some have suggested that Luther took this strong line against the peasants because of his need to have the princes on his side for the protection of the Protestant faith, but this isn't the whole story. Luther supported Catholic princes as well as Protestant ones in their attempts to put down rebellion and he said he would take the same line even if he found himself under Turkish rule.

'I am called a clergyman and am a minister of the word, but even if I served a Turk and saw my Lord in danger, I would forget my spiritual office and stab and hew as long as my heart beat.'

A more probable reason for Luther's extreme hostility to rebellion is to be found in his pessimistic view of human nature. He continually likens citizens to wild beasts held by ropes and chains. If these were released there would be nothing but biting and mangling. He argued that it is no good killing one tyrant because every citizen had five tyrants hiding within him and there is no possibility of changing things for the better. 'There is as great a difference between changing a government and improving it as the distance from heaven to earth.'

Although some Lutherans in the period after Martin Luther's death took a different attitude to the possibility of a just rebellion, in the end it was the most conservative elements in his attitude which were stressed and which became dominant in Lutheranism in the nineteenth and twentieth centuries.

Calvinism

The attitude of Calvinism to the possibility of a justified revolution is interestingly different from that of the Lutheran tradition. Martin Luther taught that the cross was at the centre of Christian life and the cross contradicted everything in the secular world. The secular world was important, was still under the rule of God, but there were no specifically Christian rules with which to order it. John Calvin (1509 – 64), by contrast, started his thinking not from the cross but from, as it were, God's point of view at the beginning of creation. Creation and redemption, Old Testament and New Testament, were all part of God's one unified plan. This meant that there were, for Calvin, revealed principles by which secular life is to be ordered and a Christian should try to ensure that he is in a position to implement them in the whole of society.

Thus Geneva, the town in Switzerland where Calvin and his party gained the upper hand, was originally planned as a little theocracy, a town whose every detail was to be guided by divine law. The town was ruled by the church, through four classes of men, pastors, doctors, elders and deacons. These men governed even people's private lives, and all pleasures such as dancing and games were forbidden.* This attitude to secular life meant that Calvinists were open to the possibility of a just revolution. Calvin himself was very cautious but he did allow for such a possibility. In a famous passage he taught that when a ruler was oppressing his people, if there were 'lesser magistrates'—senior people and bodies in the state— 'corresponding to the tribunes of old', then they should act to depose the ruler.

After Calvin Calvinism became less cautious in its attitude and Calvinist tracts advocating revolution abounded at the end of the seventeenth century. The most famous is *Vindiciae contra Tyrannos (Vengeance aginst Tyrants)*. But once again there is a note of caution against bringing about a new and worse tyranny or causing even greater evils to befall the people. The medicine may prove worse than the disease.

Calvinists take political realities seriously as a guide to what God requires of them. This has meant that when they have been in a strong minority with the chance of obtaining power they have justified revolution. When they have achieved power they have opposed revolution. This arises out of their beliefs that God is active in the whole of life and that God wants the whole of life ordered according to his will, as it has been revealed to Christians (of a Calvinist kind). Thus in South Africa, governed by Afrikaaners with a Calvinist theology, all possibility of just revolution is ruled out on religious grounds: God, through those who regard themselves as his elect, is already ordering life according to his revealed will.

---

* The nearest parallel in the twentieth century is Iran under the Ayotollah. There also the clergy have ruled and ordered the whole life of society by a book, the Qur'an. There also there has been a ban on many pleasures that western people take for granted and harsh penalties for those who disobey what is believed to be the Divine Will.

There are many forms of protestantism other than Lutheranism and Calvinism, but in their distinctive and opposed attitudes to the secular world these two Reformation traditions set the extreme limits. Lutherans say there are no distinctively Christian principles by which society is to be governed and that the ruling authority must be obeyed even if it is oppressive. Calvinists say that God has revealed in the Bible how society is to be ordered and therefore his people must try to obtain power to ensure that it is governed according to the divine will.

Questions posed by the traditions
In recent years official reports and individual writers from within both the Anglican and Lutheran traditions have been less uncompromisingly hostile to the possibility of a just revolution. But the advantage of looking at the source, where the water is clearer, is that we can see what the major emphasis has been and what it is that has shaped our own thinking. If, for example, we find that we have always been almost unthinkingly hostile to the idea of opposition to government, we can try to find out what are the cultural forces which have shaped that attitude. The traditions force certain questions on us and the attitude we take to the possibility of a just revolution depends on how we answer them.

1. Was Calvin right in his belief that the whole of human life should be shaped by the revealed will of God as recorded in the Bible? At first we are inclined to say yes. For God is indeed concered with the welfare of all human beings in all their aspects and God, being God, knows where our true good lies and how it is to be achieved. But in practice Calvinism has too often turned out to be oppressive and cruel. First, can Calvinists be certain that they have read the mind of God correctly? In South Africa they have justified apartheid on theological grounds, but Christians in other traditions

would claim that this is a misreading of the mind of God. Second, even if the mind of God is understood aright, there will be many people in any country who won't share those beliefs. A theocracy involves imposing beliefs on people whether or not the majority accept them and whether or not they are essential for the existence of human community. It is therefore a failure in the basic respect that is due to the freedom and dignity of every human being: a freedom and dignity God gives us and retains for us even when it means that we run counter to his true will. The Calvinist approach fails to do justice to the blindness, self-deception and sin of anyone who is in power (whether or not they are Calvinists) and encourages a system which does not have safeguards and checks against the abuse of power.

Calvinist theology can be dangerous. But does Lutheran theology lack something? It allows for the fact that God cares for and rules over secular life but if does not allow the Christian to bring any distinctively Christian principles to work in this area. He must just use his natural reason, motivated by love, the reason he has in common with all other men.

The use of reason, however, is a good starting point. It corresponds in part with the old Christian (and pre-Christian) idea of natural law. This assumes that all men, whatever their beliefs, are capable of coming to *some* agreement about what is right and wrong. It is a concept that used to be discredited, but in recent years it has come back in a modified form. So, we could say, a Christian trying to shape secular life will be guided by what he and other men see is the right thing to do independently of their religious point of view.

The fact that there will always be disagreement between people of good will about the kind of society they want and the kind of laws that ought to govern it is not an insuperable difficulty. For people's ideas are changing the whole time. People of all beliefs now agree about certain things which they would not have agreed on two hundred years ago, for example universal franchise and universal education.

The Christian brings to the secular world a view of man which underlines the dignity and worth of each individual. Although there may be fierce disagreements about the implications of this (e.g. on questions of abortion or euthanasia), there is a great deal of common ground with other people of good-will. The implication for one's attitude to revolution would appear to be this: a Christian will not try to bring about a revolution (or oppose a revolution) in the name of truths believed to have been revealed only to Christians. A revolution should be justified (or opposed) on grounds that will appear reasonable to all people, whatever their belief or lack of it. To argue for a revolution on the grounds that 90 per cent of the population are kept in slavery and semi-starvation is to adduce reasons that anyone capable of making moral judgments can comprehend. Similarly, to oppose an armed revolution on the grounds that it is likely to lead to a million deaths is to talk language which anyone can understand.

Lutheran theology, with its assumption that the life of society should be governed through reason and the use of moral principles shared by Christian and non-Christian alike, is not a bad starting point. It excludes fanaticism, intolerance and cruelty. But Lutheran thought over emphasised order at the expense of justice. The biblical emphasis on justice— which in an unjust world means greater justice for the poor and powerless—was neglected.

2. A second question which emerges from a study of the traditions concerns our understanding of human nature and the relationship between that understanding and our view of the state. As we have already seen, Martin Luther had a pessimistic view of man. He believed that every man had five tyrants within him. He therefore urged the necessity of a

strong state and he did not believe that a change of government changed life for the better.

In contrast to this there is the Catholic understanding of human nature and its view of the state. Catholic thought has been slightly more optimistic about human beings and has believed that even when people are not Christian believers they have some capacity to understand what is right and act on it. Arising out of this is a more positive view of the state. According to Aquinas it is natural for people to come together to order their common life, and natural for them to have some supreme authority for resolving differences. To put it in the technical shorthand of the Christian tradition: the state is not just the result of, and a remedy for, the sin brought about by the fall of man (as it is understood in Lutheran thought). It is a natural institution which belongs to man's life in the paradise of Eden. The element of coercion has been made essential by man's sin but government itself is part of our unfallen condition. The implication of these different views of man and their corresponding attitude to the state is crucial for our beliefs about the rightness or wrongness of revolution. On a Lutheran view any attempt to overthrow government by force would at best be pointless and at worst it would release anarchy or bring about an even worse tyranny. It could achieve nothing good and it would risk greater harm. On the Catholic view, with its more optimistic view of man and the state, the state exists to develop good possibilities as well as to check human sin. On this view we could rightly expect the state to order the common life for the good of all. If it failed to do so by becoming tyrannical then we would look for the overthrow of one regime and the installation of a new one which could, to some degree, improve the lot of the subjects.

The Lutheran view of man and the state, in a milder non-theological form, is very much part of the English consciousness. But is it a correct view? Real changes for the better *do* take place. In the great film by the Italian director Olmi, *The Tree of the Wooden Clogs* we observe the life of some peasant families in the north of Italy during the nineteenth century. It is not a film of political propaganda. We enter into the lives of individuals as individuals and their relationships with one another. Yet those individuals cannot be seen apart from the social and political forces which shape their lives.

First, they are tenants with no rights, under an obligation to give a large part of their produce to the landowner. The climax of the film (and also its end) occurs when one family is evicted, with nowhere to go and no money, because the father cut down a tree to make some clogs for his child to wear on his journey to school. Second, education is regarded as the exception and not for them. The parish priest has to put pressure on the father to allow his boy, who is exceptionally bright, to go to school. Third, the families are supported by their religion whch pervades all they do.

It is quite clear that the social and political conditions in which we now live and which shape our lives, are very different from those. Tenants have rights, everyone has to go to school, religion does not play such a large part. These changes are either for the better or for the worse. They are not neutral. They radically affect the fulfilment and happiness of individual beings and therefore they matter, to God and to us.

People sometimes suggest that Christians ought to be indifferent to the kind of government that they live under. It is true that a Christian might have to live under any kind of government, and that the Christian life can and must be lived out even under an anti-religious system such as communism, but this is very different from saying that all governments are equally good or bad. It matters what kind of government people have to live under, because governments affect people's individual lives for good or ill. Furthermore, a Christian can rightly look to a government to order the common life for the common good, and this will include a great deal more than the suppression of crime and the maintenance of order. Therefore might not a Christian have to consider seriously the possibility of armed revolution if a government is manifestly tyrannical and there is no democratic means available of changing it?

3. The third point raised by a study of the traditions concerns the influence of political considerations on ethical ideas. In the early church Christians did not even consider the possibility of a just rebellion because their need was recognition and peace within the already existing political system. In the sixteenth and seventeenth centuries churchmen in emerging nation-states of Protestant belief wished to achieve national unity round the sovereign. Churchmen in other countries of Catholic persuasion wished to achieve the unity of Christendom round the Pope. There were two different concepts of unity. The one had, for political reasons, to disallow any possibility of just rebellion. The other, for political reasons (where there were Catholics in a Protestant country), could allow such a possibility.

This is an old example of a problem that is still with us, though the political considerations are now related not to religion but to economics. Those with a large stake in the status-quo will tend to be hostile to the concept of a just revolution. Those on the margins of society will be sympathetic to it. This could make one cynical about considering the question of revolution in ethical terms at all. But it need not. It could make one ask more searchingly about the criteria which have to be fulfilled if a revolution is to be regarded as just, and look more honestly at particular situations to see if the criteria are met. We shall consider these criteria in later chapters.

3
Violence and the modern world

Institutional violence

People sometimes blame communists for the amount of political violence there is in the modern world. It is important therefore to take a cool, clear look to see exactly what is the role of violence in communist theory.

1. There was no great emphasis on the role of violence in the thought of Karl Marx (1818 – 83). For him history was a series of *economic* revolutions. Each age, according to him, has its own particular economic order. As man develops new skills this order is put under pressure to change. So, in Europe in the middle ages there was an agricultural society, characterised by a sharp division between the nobility and the peasant classes. As an agricultural society began to give way to an industrial one, the commercial classes, enterpreneurs, factory owners, managers and so on, became larger and more powerful. They became the dominant class, as they are in many countries today. Marx believed that this process of economic change would continue and that a society in which the workers were the predominant class would eventually come about. Finally there would be a communist or classless society.

According to Marx the pressure to change from one kind of society to another, and therefore from one governing class to another, came primarily from economic factors. Furthermore, this change took place almost automatically. There was an inevitability about it. If this picture is borne in mind it is easy to understand why orthodox communist parties in the modern world have often been regarded as conservative by other left wing groups. During the student riots in Paris in 1968, for example, the communist party stood aside, critical of what was going on. Likewise in South America communist parties are often to be found arguing for caution. This is because according to Marxist theory the change to a socialist society (one in which the workers are the predominant group) will be almost automatic. When the right moment comes only a little push will be needed.

So there is no great emphasis in Marx himself on violence, but clearly the Marxist framework, in which society is seen as a process of continuous economic change, with one ruling group giving way to another, provides a framework in which others can urge the necessity of violence in order to speed up the process. That is what has in fact happened. Regis Debray, a modern French writer, building on the experience of Castro, who with a small army gained control of Cuba, has stressed the urgency of the task of bringing about revolutionary change. Instead of waiting for just the right conditions to emerge revolutionaries must take arms and bring about a revolutionary situation. So, as Regis Debray put it at the end of an influential book, 'That is why *insurrectional activity is today the number one political activity.'*

Although Marx himself did not stress the role of revolutionary violence in effecting change, there is one aspect of his thought which is particularly pervasive in the modern world—his understanding of the state. He makes two main points. First, the fact that we need a state, that is, an apparatus of government with its judiciary, legislature, civil services, police and army, is a reflection of the fact that human society is in a state of alienation. Men are alienated from themselves, their work and one another, because society is still divided into classes. When a classless society has been achieved the state will just 'wither away'. Although there will still be the need for some degree of organisation and administration there will be no necessity for coercive force to achieve the communal good.

2. Until the arrival of a classless or communist society the state always represents the interests of a particular ruling class. In Marx's time the whole apparatus of state was, according to him, in the hands of the bourgeoisie who used it to further their own interests. 'The Executive of the modern state is but a committee for managing the common affairs of the bourgeoisie,' he wrote in the *Communist Manifesto*. And again, 'The state is an organisation of violence for the suppression of some class.' In a socialist society, the society which leads up to and prepares the way for a communist society, the state is still very much with us: during this period instead of serving the interests of the bourgeois class it serves the cause of the workers.

In Russia Lenin put this theory into practice. Through a combination of ruthless singlemindedness and sheer luck he seized power in 1917 and continued his previous policy of refusing to allow any opposition to his views. A small revolutionary élite setting out to make the state serve the interests of the workers eventually controlled every aspect of government. According to Lenin the state was 'organised and systematic violence'. The difference was that now the violence was being used on behalf of the workers instead of the property owners.

It is from this Marxist-Leninist understanding of the state that the concept of 'institutional violence' is derived. According to that standpoint a non-communist state will always protect the interests of the bourgeois members by all methods that are necessary. Those who challenge the state will soon experience its violence for themselves. Thus, one of the aims of committed Marxists in big rallies or demonstrations is to achieve a confrontation with the police in which the police are shown using violence. In this way they hope to convince others that beneath the state's leather glove is a cruel claw. Furthermore, if a group takes to armed revolution this will be seen as a *defensive* reaction to the state. For the Capitalist state, according to Marxist-Leninist theory, is already exercising violence against its workers.

People brought up in western-style democracies and taught that the state is neutral, serving impartially the interests of all its citizens, find this concept of 'institutional volence' alien and unconvincing. So, we have to recognise that there is *some* truth in it. (To admit that there is some truth in certain Marxist beliefs carries us no way towards becoming Marxists. Even the conservative historian Dr Edward Norman has said, 'Aspects of Marxist social analysis are extremely valuable!') In a democratic society, although everyone has the vote and anyone could in theory stand for power or form a new party, in practice achieving a position of power takes money. Obviously, people who own the wealth of the country will want, like anyone else, to further their own interests. They will try to ensure that they have a government that represents their point of view and they will make their money available to further this end. Once their men or women have achieved power then the apparatus of government, including the police and the army, are at the service of policies which protect their interests.

In England and most of America people are fortunate. There are at least two parties with access to a regular income and with a real chance of achieving power. There are institutions such as an independent judiciary, a non-political army and many laws safeguarding rights, which go a great way towards making the system a fair one.

Furthermore, even if we grant that there is some truth in the Marxist understanding of the state and agree that western democracies, despite all safeguards, show a bias to the wealthy, there is still the spectre of Russian communism to weigh against this. The practical working out of the Marxist-Leninist idea of the state put at the service of the workers, is there for all to see. 27 million people were killed in the great purges in the 1920s and 1930s, and terrible massacres still take place in some countries where Marxists have gained control. In this world it is never a question of choosing between a perfect system and a bad one but between one that is imperfect and others that are even more imperfect. As Reinhold Niebuhr put it, 'Democracy is the worst possible system in the world—except for all the others.'

The democratic system itself is not violent, or to put it more accurately, it is less violent than alternative ones. So it is more accurate to say that the state exercises a degree of force (rather than violence) both in order to maintain internal control and as a protection against external enemies. The word force refers to the moral and legally authorised use of such coercion as is strictly necessary. The word violence refers to coercion or threats of coercion that are immoral, illegal or excessive.

On a Christian understanding of man, in which we know ourselves to be less than perfect, with a capacity for brutality as well as love, it is necessary to have governments with the power to coerce as well as persuade. There is no moral justification for taking up arms against a genuine democracy, that is, one in which it is possible to replace one government by another through elections in which everyone has the vote, simply on the grounds that the state is 'organised violence'. A state may be imperfect, it may express the interests of one class or group more than another, but in so far as there is the possibility of changing the government by ballot it still possesses a legitimate use of force.

Liberating violence
For Marx and Lenin violence had a purely instrumental character, that is, they valued it as a means to achieve a desired

end. But in the 1960s another attitude came to the fore, which regarded violence as personally liberating. The twentieth century roots of this go back to a Frenchman, Georges Sorel (1847 – 1922). Sorel taught the necessity of a mass, spontaneous uprising of all workers to seize the means of production. He believed that this action, which he compared to a heroic military venture, would actually help to change and liberate those who took part in it. This great mass action would not just transform the state but would transform the individual lives of those who shared its risks.

Sorel would probably have been forgotten except for the influence he is believed to have had on Franz Fanon who became prominent during the Algerian War of Independence. Fanon was born in Martinique and qualified as a psychiatrist in France. In a series of books and articles he explored the role of violence in colonialism and the anti-colonialist struggles. In the race riots in America in 1967 a journalist was told, 'Every brother on a roof top can quote Fanon', and a report on a guerilla band in Bolivia contained the words, 'The newest thing about it was its intense demonstration of belief in violence as a virtuous action. . . . One of their favourite books had been Franz Fanon's *The Wretched of the Earth*.' In that book Fanon showed how violence played a crucial role in all anti-colonialist struggles. Moderate leaders, for example, always made use of the threat of the violence of people less moderate than themselves. They said, in effect, 'You had better settle with me now. Look at the men of violence and think how much worse it will be if they get into power.' Violence may win a struggle but often it is the moderates who reap the rewards.

Fanon's other main point, however, is much more controversial. He maintained that the violence used in the struggle for independence helped people to find personal liberation. 'At the level of individuals violence is a cleansing force,' he wrote. Again, 'Violence is thus seen as comparable to a royal pardon. The colonised man finds his freedom in and through violence.' Violence was necessary not just to liberate people from colonial rule but to liberate them personally from the psychological effects of that rule.

We see in Fanon a strong humanist strand, the necessity of people to stand up for themselves, which we have already asserted to be a properly Christian concept. We see also the influence of his psychiatric training with its emphasis on the necessity, from the health point of view, of expressing strong emotions rather than repressing them. This emphasis is a valuable one when the expression is verbal. But when the violence is physical, the psychological effect can be far from healthy, as Fanon himself points out in other contexts. His study of those who carried out torture in Algeria showed how they became dehumanised and insensitive in every area of their life.

Fanon wrote, 'Let us decide not to imitate Europe . . . Let us try to create the whole man, whom Europe has been incapable of bringing to birth.' He said that when he looked for man in Europe all he saw was 'an avalanche of murders'. But this is precisely what occurred in the Algerian war. No doubt Algeria could have obtained her independence only by the use of force, but this did not create 'the whole man' and it did not bring personal liberation to those who took part in the violent struggle. On the contrary, the extent of the violence was dehumanising to all concerned.

During the 1970s the trend in the west was away from the previous emphasis on violence. For example, Eldridge Cleaver, the founder of the Black Panthers in America, a group that asserted the necessity of violence, in contrast to the different methods of Martin Luther King, has become a Christian and a believer in reconciliation. He eschews his former methods, and in a rally at Birmingham, England, in September 1979 he urged any of the crowd who had a hatred for policemen to shake hands with the officers on patrol. But the attitude to violence characterised by Fanon is always likely to recur. The use of arms comes to be seen not just as a necessary evil, but good in itself. But when we use violence against another human being we have to become insensitive to the humanity they share with us. It means blotting out their human face from our consciousness. The result is that rather than becoming liberated we turn ourselves spiritually to stone.

Liberation Theology

One of the Christian responses to the emphasis on revolutionary change has been Liberation Theology. It first came to prominence in an essay by Roger Shaull, an American theologian, who argued that God was ceaselessly at work in his world breaking down dehumanising structures. Christians, according to Shaull, were to discern where God was at work liberating humanity and to co-operate with him in his work. Since then Liberation Theology has been associated particularly with a number of theologians in South America. There is a wide range of writers and ideas but a few points may be singled out as fundamental.

First, theology is always related either unconsciously or consciously to the socio-political situation in which it is done. More often than not the relationship is unconscious, so that a theology which thinks of itself as uttering timeless truths does in fact reflect the values of a particular age, class or country. These unconscious assumptions need to be exposed. Second, theology then needs to be related consciously to the needs of those people who, above all, are in the heart of God, the poor and the oppressed.

These are important points. For example, those who stress a theology of reconciliation do not always realise that this is related to their situation as people who have some stake in the status quo of their society. The language of reconciliation does not seem so obviously the word of God to people who are oppressed and who know that confrontation and change must precede and prepare the way for genuine reconciliation. Further, the word of God, if it is truly the word of God that is being uttered, will indeed speak to the condition of the poor and oppressed. According to the gospels their poverty may enable them to hear the gospel, when the riches of others prevent them from hearing. Moreover the gospel seems to hold out special hope to the poor, just because they are poor.

Nevertheless it has to be said that fundamental theological truths, although they arise out of particular human societies and have to be spoken to particular societies, are enduring; they are truths that can be apprehended as truth in every time and every place. The Christian understanding of God as Father, Son and Holy Spirit, three persons in one God, is true for all people at all times in all places. The relationship between these theological beliefs and the needs of people in particular societies is not a matter of theology but of *ethics*. Christian beliefs have political implications but they are not themselves political statements.

Another stress in Liberation Theology, as the phrase indicates, is that God is liberating mankind from all that enslaves us. Liberation theologians tend to look to the Old Testament, to the rescue of the people of Israel from bondage in Egypt and the liberation of the people later from captivity in Babylon. But the same theme is strongly present in the New Testament. When Christ went into the synagogue at Capernaum he read the famous passage from Isaiah,

'The Spirit of the Lord is upon me,
because he has anointed me to preach good news to the poor.
He has sent me to proclaim release to the captives
and recovering of sight to the blind,
to set at liberty those who are oppressed,
to proclaim the acceptable year of the Lord.'
And he began to say to them 'Today this scripture has been fulfilled in your hearing' (Luke 4: 18ff).

Both the Old and the New Testaments show God at work liberating us from all that enslaves us. But it is not always obvious to us what human agencies he is using to do his work. Imagine a country where government has collapsed completely and the inhibitants hardly dare go out on the street for fear of attack by marauding gangs, where they don't know if there will be food in the shops tomorrow even if they are lucky enough to find some today. In that country a political party that had as its main policy the restoration of order could rightly be regarded as liberating. For true order brings freedom. It gives us freedom to predict the future and so to plan our activities. We know there will be food in the shops tomorrow; so today, instead of queuing up, we can visit a friend. On the way to that friend we won't be attacked. Or suppose that in the same country there are two other political parties, both of which promised not only to restore order but to obtain a better deal for the poorest sections of the community. One of these is explicitly Marxist and the other Social Democratic. Which is the genuinely liberating force? Here *political* and *ethical* judgment is required. An emphasis on the liberation which God is bringing does not give us automatic insight into which agency is bringing that liberation about.

The intention of liberation theologies is a laudable one. They wish to make a much closer connection between Christian reflection about God and Christian action. They want to bind them so tight that you could not have the one without the other. Further, there is the good intention of showing that Christian theology must lead to political commitment on behalf of the poor. But, as already indicated, between Christian theology and Christian action there must be ethical and political reflection.

Christian action in the world arises out of a recognition of God's nature as love and a desire to respond to it. To take just one example, when Paul wanted to urge his readers to humility, he reminded them of the humility of the divine incarnation in Jesus. Coming to recognise that God loves us, we want to respond to this by loving our fellow human beings, made in his image. Love for neighbour, as everyone knows, is the basic Christian ethical teaching. But this directive does not of itself tell us just what is, in any particular situation, the most loving action. To love someone means that we have in the front of our minds their well-being, their good. But exactly what their well-being consists of, and how it is to be achieved, are questions where answers are far from obvious. It opens up the whole field of moral and political philosophy as well as of Christian ethics.

It is true that some people have a kind of instinct for what is the most loving thing to do, and in many situations involving personal relationships we have 'to play it by ear', relying on our intuition. But working out what is the most loving course of action in controversial areas of personal and social ethics requires as much hard thought as we can give it.

None of this should suggest that a Christian can be politically uncommitted. On the contrary, you cannot love your neighbour in the modern world without being involved in one way or another with politics. The point need not be laboured. Christian love for neighbour has to be expressed in the political sphere as well as the personal one. One way of thinking about the relationship between the personal and the political is to think of love being concerned with the whole person, including the needs unique to him, and justice being concerned with the needs that we all have in common. For example, I have certain personal needs, like reading or going to the theatre. Others need to hear good music or watch football. But we all need to eat and we all need a roof over our heads. Politics is concerned with order, freedom and justice— the needs we have in common. The way the Christian tries to meet these needs is through political thought and action. This is how he loves his neighbour.

These considerations which have been discussed in relation to God's love for us and our answering recognition of this love apply in just the same way to the idea of God as the liberator. To say that God is actively liberating mankind from all that enslaves us is just to underline one aspect of what it means to say he loves us. We are still required to build a bridge from theology to action. This is provided by ethical and political reflection. We recognise that God is liberating mankind and we wish to respond by sharing in this work of liberation. But we still have to work out what this liberation means and what are the best, or least evil, means of attaining that liberation for a particular group.

This chapter has considered two approaches to violence that are current in the modern world. The first, characterised by the phrase Institutional Violence, implies that the state is by definition a violent structure and that violent acts against it are thereby justified. But though no state is entirely neutral we argued that all states need to make use of some coercive power and that this is legitimate. In the case of political systems which allowed for change of government by normal democratic means violence against the state could not be justified simply on the grounds that the state itself is using force.

The second approach, characterised by the phrase Liberation Theology, suggests that God is ceaselessly at work in his world liberating people from all that oppresses them. He is. But we still have to ask where he is at work and through what human agencies he is working. A bridge has to be built from theological beliefs to the right action by ethical and political wisdom. When it comes to the moral rightness or wrongness of taking up arms against the state much of this wisdom is contained in the Just Revolution tradition.

4
What makes a just revolution just?

Legitimate Authority

The body of thinking by Christians who have believed that war can sometimes be justified is called the 'just war tradition'. According to this a war is considered to be just only if it is authorised by those in a proper position to make such a judgement. In the modern world this means the government of a country. Inside a country, if a dispute arises between groups or individuals, they can apply to the courts and in England, for example, in the last analysis appeal to the House of Lords. There is a higher authority who will settle the dispute. But in a quarrel between countries there is no higher authority to settle it. The United Nations ought to be able to do this but it can't. It can make judgements about who is right, but as at present constituted it does not have the power to enforce those judgements.

This means that if all else fails the government of a country has the right to wage a defensive war to protect its people. It and only it, has the authority to declare a state of war. This obviously poses a big problem for those whose sense of justice is leading them to take up arms against their own government. How can such an act possibly be authorised? And if it is not properly authorised then it fails to meet the first criterion of the just war tradition.

Two points can be made. First, as stated in chapter one, it is possible for a state to usurp the position of God and so become demonic. In that case it ceases to be the state described by Paul in Romans 13 and it has no moral claim on

Christians. This happened in Nazi Germany when Hitler put the state and its immoral laws in place of God. Such a state no longer has any authority, whatever it may claim.

Second, all government depends in the end on consent. Even in a police state it is necessary to obtain the consent of some people, the secret police for example. A government with true authority is one that has the consent of its people, though in practice this means the consent of the majority of its people. A government has power over its people and it governs in their name. It must therefore have received a mandate from them. What happens in a potentially revolutionary situation is that a government continues to cling to power long after the people have in fact withdrawn their consent. It holds power because it controls the police and the army but in fact the government is no longer authorised. In order for a revolution to be accounted just this point must have been reached. When it has been reached the revolution is not one against 'lawfully constituted authority' because the government no longer has an authority.

The difficulty in practice, of course, is to judge when this point has been reached. But we had one dramatic example in 1979 in the Iranian revolution, which shows that the criteria do have meaning. The Shah appeared to be the authorised ruler. He had a vast army and a powerful police force. Set against him was the voice of Ayotollah Khomeini, a resurgent Islam and the discontent of people. It became apparent in a very short time that the people had withdrawn their consent from the Shah's government and given it to the Ayotollah. There was a great deal of unrest and much minor skirmishing, but compared to many other revolutions it was relatively free from bloodshed. The main reason was the fact that the vast majority of the people had withdrawn their mandate from the Shah and vested the Ayotollah with authority. This rapidly became obvious to the Shah and his supporters who failed to control the country despite the large army.

The Iranian example is a clearer one than most situations allow. Elsewhere the scene is usually one of confusion. It may not be absolutely apparent that the people have withdrawn their consent from the government in power and there may be several opposition groups each claiming authority.

This emphasis on the need for authority even by those starting a revolution may seem surprising, but this is because a true revolution is always made in the name of a better order as well as of a greater justice. Anarchic revolution is totally ruled out by the Christian just war and just revolution tradition. On the Christian view of man government is necessary and even in the chaotic conditions produced by a revolution one must look for a group who will emerge with the power to achieve a new order. Those writers in the Christian tradition, both Catholic and Calvinist, who have allowed the possibility of a just revolution, all stressed that the revolution must be carried out by the leading men and institutions of the state. The intention behind this emphasis, rather than its literal application, is what is important. The intention is that the revolution be an ordered revolution, in the name of a better order, and not mere anarchy.

For a revolutionary movement to be accounted just, therefore, it must first be established that the state has become demonic (as it did under Hitler); or that the existing government, although it continues to hold on to power through the use of coercion, has in fact had its mandate withdrawn by the people, as happened in Iran. Further, there must be some alternative authority which either already holds the allegiance of the mass of the people, as the Ayotollah appeared to do, or who can obtain power, establish order and have its actions subsequently ratified by the people as a whole, as happened in Angola and Mozambique. Order is as essential to a society as justice.

Just cause

It is obvious that if a revolution is to be regarded as justified the cause must be just. It is equally obvious that all those who make revolution believe that their cause *is* just. But is it really? Writers in the just war/just revolution tradition have always emphasised as strongly as they could that resort to arms must be a last resort. Every other means of obtaining redress must first have been tried. On the question of revolution, in particular, it has been stressed that the tyranny must be long standing and manifest. Writers have pointed out all the dangers of increased repression and social upheaval that are risked by attempts to remove tyrannical governments. All these factors have to be taken into account when deciding if there is a just cause.

The principle of proportion

The principle of proportion states that the evil unleashed by fighting must not outweight the good that will be achieved. Or, to put it another way, the evil unleashed must be less than the evil that is being endured under the tyranny. In short, the cost must be counted, consequences must be taken into account and assessed. This principle, as already mentioned in chapter two, first appears as a formal principle of Christian ethics in Aquinas' discussion of sedition.

Stated in general terms the principle of proportion appears so vague as to be useless. For example, are we to consider only casualties, the number of people killed or wounded? Or are we to consider spiritual values as well, like loss of personal freedom under a tyranny? The fact is that when people weigh the consequences of acting in a particular way they very rarely limit their thinking to the number of possible casualties. Those who fought the Nazis were thinking of the deprivation to the human spirit that would result from Nazi control, not just of the physical suffering that would have ensued. People who rose against the Russians in Prague in 1968 and those who demonstrated in Soweto in South Africa were concerned for more than human suffering of a physical kind—they were concerned for the dignity and freedom of the human spirit. But once we allow values like freedom to be taken into account there is almost no loss that could not be justified in the name of a greater freedom or justice. Although this is theoretically true and has sometimes proved true in practice, counting the consequences does in fact act as a check on some occasions. For example, according to the predominant set of values in America the people of eastern Europe are living in slavery, and since the second world war America has seen it as part of its foreign policy to protect those who share their own value system. But not at any price. America did not intervene to help the Czech uprising in 1968. It did not intervene to stop the Russian oppression in Hungary in 1956. It could have done so only at the risk of a nuclear war. It was not prepared to pay that price.

The principle of proportion first came to prominence in the work of the great Spanish writer Francisco de Vitoria (1480 – 1546). He was appalled by the destruction that the Spaniards were wreaking on the Indians in South America. He argued that however just their cause might be, the cost in terms of human suffering was so great that their fighting was not morally justified. The good that Vitoria had in mind was both the good of the Indians and the wider good. 'If any war should be advantageous to one province or nation but injurious to the world or to Christendom, it is my belief that, for this very reason, that war is unjust.'

This is a principle of vital importance, even more so in civil strife than in war between countries. For civil wars can be devastating in the cost to human life and the human spirit over many generations. We think of Spain, not just the enormous number of casualties during the civil war but the legacy of Fascism and bitterness that the war left. We reflect on what has happened in Russia and what could happen in

South Africa. It is possible for a populace to have a just cause, the tyranny being manifest and of long standing, with every peaceful means to obtain change explored and found to be of no avail—and still it could be that resort to arms would not be morally justified, for the cost to human life and the human spirit would be too enormous. But obviously the principle of proportion is closely linked to the possible outcome of the revolution. For if the revolution is going to fail anyway, human suffering will have been caused to no avail.

So the Spanish theologian, Suarez, referred to in chapter two, was right to say that for fighting to be justified there must be a reasonable prospect of success. Suarez argued that a weaker force would never be justified in making war upon a stronger, however just its cause. A ruler 'ought at least to have either a more probable expectation of victory or one equally balanced as to the chances of victory or defeat, and that, in proportion to the need of the state and the communal welfare.'

Although writers in the non-catholic traditions do not have formal criteria for what constitutes a just war or just revolution many do in fact follow a similar way of thinking. For example, Martin Luther had no illusions about the horror of war: 'War is one of the greatest plagues that can afflict humanity . . . Any scourge, in fact, is preferable to it. Famine and pestilence become as nothing in comparison of it.' In view of this it is not surprising that he urges extreme caution and a great state of preparedness before a war is undertaken. He was strongly critical of King Louis of Hungary who went into battle against the Turks with an army of thirty thousand to face an army of one hundred thousand, and he wrote 'If we are not going to make an adequate, honest resistance that will have some reserve power, it would be far better not to begin a war, but to yield land and people to the Turk in time, without useless bloodshed, rather than have him win anyhow

in an easy battle with shameful bloodshed.' So strongly did
Luther feel about this that he said he would rather have a bad
man who was prudent as a ruler than a good man who was
imprudent.

We should not expect the criterion that there must be a
reasonable chance of success to have a place in Calvinism,
which thinks in terms of war being sanctioned by the holy
will of God and that alone. But in fact Calvin and the
Calvinist tracts which advocated revolution on the continent
rated human prudence highly as did Cromwell and Milton in
England in the seventeenth century. Christopher Hill has
written about Cromwell, 'For Oliver "waiting on provi-
dences" meant making absolutely sure that the political
situation was ripe before taking drastic action—ensuring that
the army and his leaders were with him and that the city
would acquiesce.'

In both Catholic and non-catholic thought part of the
process of *moral* decision making is taking a hard look at the
situation and assessing the consequences of possible courses of
action. Some people think that moral decisions are ones that
are made according to some principle—like stealing is
wrong—and that assessing the consequences of an action and
letting your decision be affected by the calculation is something that has nothing to do with morality. People sometimes
call taking the consequences into account expediency, the
word being used to express disapproval. On the other hand
there are some people for whom such calculation is what
making moral decision is all about. Where war and revolution
are concerned Christian Ethics are more complex. Certain
actions are judged to be wrong in all circumstances
(deliberately killing a harmless civilian, for example), but
calculation of consequences plays an essential part as well.

There must, then, be a reasonable chance of success before a
revolutionary action can be regarded as morally justified. But
before applying this principle it is essential to ask what it is

that a revolution is trying to achieve. What counts as success? In his widely read study of revolutionary wars, *The War of the Flea,* Robert Tabor argued that the purpose of a revolutionary force was not to win victories but to *stay in existence.* Revolutionary war is primarily political war. It is, to adopt the maxim of the military thinker, Clauswitz, the extension of politics by other means. By staying in existence and posing a threat, a revolutionary army forces the government to spend an ever increasing amount of money on military measures. It seeks to be a continuing nuisance, whilst at the same time carrying out a propaganda war. Tabor examines his thesis in relation to all the wars of liberation that have taken place since the second world war and shows how the policy was successfully applied in country after country. Where it was not used, in Greece, the revolutionary group failed to win. 'In the Greek context, the revolutionary principle bears repetition: the object of the guerilla is not to win battles, but to avoid defeat, not to end the war but to prolong it, until political victory, more important than battlefield victory, has been won.'

Those few writers who have used the criteria of the just revolution tradition to discuss modern liberation movements seem to have been unaware of this point. For example, the Catholic John Epstein, writing in 1972 about the liberation movement then operating in Portuguese territories, wrote, 'On the evidence of the last decade they have no reasonable prospect of success at all'. For this and other reasons he did not regard their cause as morally justified. Yet in 1974 the Portuguese empire in Africa collapsed and these same liberation movements triumphed. It was another dramatic illustration of Tabor's thesis, for no decisive military victory had been won. The guerilla armies had stayed in existence, constituting a continual threat and an increasing drain on the Portuguese treasury. At the same time the political battle was being fought and, in the end, won.

The size of the guerilla force does not matter. General Grivas began in Cyprus with 80 men; Fidel Castro in Cuba with a handful. The only thing that matters is whether there is a bitter and long-standing grievance. Given this, continuing guerilla activity, on however small a scale, is likely within the foreseeable future to galvanise the whole population and world opinion against an oppressive regime. The English or American Christian, who looks at liberation movements in various parts of the world and wonders if, as a Christian, he ought to support them, will consider first the nature of the tyranny. Is it long-standing and manifest? Has every peaceful means of exchange been explored? Second, he will ask if there is a revolutionary force with the potential to stay in existence long enough for the political battle to be won.

Where we stand

The argument of this book should now be clear. There can be such a thing as a just revolution, *provided that certain criteria are fulfilled.* In order to decide whether these criteria have been fulfilled it is necessary to take a realistic look at the political situation in question and to do some hard-headed calculations about the consequences of possible courses of action.

We now come up against an enormous difficulty. How we weigh the consequences depends so much on where we stand in the society being considered. To take a simple analogy. A person precariously balanced on the top of a pile of logs is aware of the hurt that will be done to him if it collapses. Not surprisingly he calls out for stability, for change that is gentle. A person who is squashed under the pile of logs, however, is conscious of his present hurt. He calls out to be freed from his pain. He doesn't want the whole pile to collapse but he can see that it may be inevitable if he is going to get free of the weight that is crushing him.

It is easy to understand how those sitting beside their swimming pools in Johannesburg are fearful of the great hurt that they are likely to suffer if society is shaken up. Inevitably they talk about the need for stability, for order. Those who live in Crossroads, however, or in other townships which are being razed to the ground as part of the policy of apartheid, know only the present pain. They call for freedom and justice. South Africa's problem is not fundamentally a racialist one. The determining forces are economic. Apartheid is a means of preserving the white minority in power and wealth. This is why the English speaking community are so ineffective in bringing about real change. Though many English speaking people have non-racial attitudes and belong to groups that are racially mixed, like those which come together in church and liberal circles, the fact is that the English speaking community benefits economically from apartheid just as much as the Afrikaaner community. This is the main reason for the slow rate of change.

This raises the question of the 'liberal', whether he is a Christian, Jew or agnostic. His position in society is not usually either at the top or the bottom. Analysing his attitude from a socio-political point of view it is easy to say that his liberal attitudes spring from a combination of fear that the whole society will collapse, in which case he too has much to lose, and some sympathy for the pain of those who are oppressed and deprived. But this easy analysis, though true from one point of view, misses the essential point. In 'liberal' attitudes there is something essential to our humanity. The Marxist believes that everything is determined by economic factors and that values are simply the surface froth of such forces. The liberal believes that values, though they are rooted in human societies, have an independent validity.

There is something essential to human community and being a human being in ideas like order, freedom and justice. There is often a connection between a particular value and a particular class, as there was between freedom and the rising bourgeoisie in the seventeenth, eighteenth and nineteenth centuries in Europe, for freedom from feudal ties of various kinds furthered the interests of business and commerce. But freedom is basic to the human spirit of all classes of all peoples. The liberal, therefore, whilst aware of the economic factors, will not agree that everything is completely determined by them. He will look at a particular situation as objectively as he can, as rationally as possible. However difficult this is, however difficult it is to foresee the future and to weigh probable or possible consequences one against the other, he will try. In Campuchia, as a result of the fighting in recent years, nearly 4 million people out of a population of 8 million have perished. No value, whether of order, justice or freedom could justify or outweigh such human suffering. Almost any lack of order or justice or freedom should be put up with rather than risk the chance of inflicting such suffering. Being rational and objective does not mean ignoring economic factors or disregarding the plight of particular groups or classes. It means taking them into account. But it involves taking many other factors into consideration as well.

In order for a revolutionary attempt to be morally justified certain criteria must be met. It must have moral authorisation in the sense indicated earlier. There must be a just cause and this means that every peaceful means of obtaining change must first have been explored. The likely suffering as the result of the fighting must be less than that endured under the oppressive regime. This carries the implication that there must be a reasonable chance of winning. This does not mean winning battles so much as staying in existence as a continuing nuisance until the political victory is won.

All these criteria make it essential to examine carefully the actual situation and to do some hard-headed calculation of what might be possible within it. This is a minimal duty for Christian and non-Christian alike.

5
Terrorism—is anything permitted?

The feature of guerilla warfare that worries people more than any other is often called terrorism. This is not a particularly useful word as terror is an aspect of all warfare and the word itself does not indicate whether it is soldiers or civilians who are being terrorised. In fact, when people talk about terrorism and describe freedom fighters as terrorists, they are usually thinking of attacks on civilians. Such people often feel that wars of liberation are immoral in a way that wars between countries are not, because such wars so often involve terrorism against the civilian population. It is right to be worried about the possibility of this happening for both the end we want to achieve and the means we select to achieve it need to be morally justifiable. But there are two separate moral issues. In other words it is possible to say that particular people are justified in fighting for their freedom but that the means which they are using are immoral. Or, on the other hand, it is possible to say that they are fighting without proper cause but that their conduct of the campaign has been moral.

Some people believe that once a revolution has broken out any means can be used to further it, or, if one is opposed to the revolution, any means can be used to end it. They deny that there is a moral dimension to the means used in warfare. So a columnist writing about the 'Green Berets', who were accused of immoral conduct during the war in Vietnam, argued that this was hypocrisy. 'A war, whether or not the cause be "just", licenses thuggery.' But the tradition of Christian thinking on these matters has never seen it like that.

For Christian writers there must not only be just cause, but the means used to fight the war or revolution must be moral as well.

The main moral principle to be observed is that there must be no direct attacks on civilians who are not directly contributing to the war effort. This is sometimes called the principle of discrimination, or the principle of non-combatant immunity. We will look briefly at its origin, consider whether it should still have a place in our thinking and then ask the question whether revolutions must inevitably break this principle.

The origin of this principle has been traced to the peace movements of the tenth and eleventh centuries. The population, tired of the ceaseless bloodshed of the feudal wars, combined with the Church to make certain classes of men immune from direct attack by other Christians. In 1095 Pope Urban II said that priests, pilgrims and merchants, for example, were to be immune from direct attack. A later Church council offered the same protection to serfs and olive trees. But it was with the sixteenth century Spanish Dominican, Fransisco de Vitoria, who has already been mentioned, that the immunity of non-combatants from direct attack became a formal moral principle. He took Aquinas' teaching that the innocent should never be killed and applied it to war, interpreting it to mean that all those not directly contributing to the war effort should not be the object of direct attack.

Here is an example of a theme that runs all through Vitoria's writings on war. 'The deliberate slaughter of the innocent is never lawful in itself. Hence it follows that even in war with the Turks it is not allowable to kill children. This is clear because they are innocent. Aye, and the same holds for women of unbelievers. This is clear, because so far as the war is concerned, they are presumed innocent; but it does not hold in the case of any individual woman who is certainly guilty.'

48

In other words, it is not civilians *per se* who are immune but civilians who are not engaged in the fighting. A village containing only women and children should not be the object of direct attack. But to take a modern example, if one of the women is found to have a grenade under her blouse she can be prevented from throwing it by the usual means. Vitoria points out that many civilians will unfortuntely be hurt as a result of attacks on military targets in populated areas. If a fortified town which has a garrison and guns is attacked then of course many civilians are going to be injured or killed. But they are not the direct object of attack and their deaths are not intended. Here the principle of proportion discussed in chapter four applies. The cost in terms of human suffering has to be weighed against the possible military advantage.

The immunity of non-combatants from direct attack was taught by Grotius (1583 – 1645), the great founder of International Law, and it has found its way into international laws and conventions. It has also come to be part of the military law of many countries. It was by this principle, expressed in terms of military law, that, the American, Lt. Calley, was brought to trial for killing civilians in Vietnam.

So although it is easy to understand those who feel that, once a war has broken out, 'anything goes', Christian writers have never taken this view. In the modern world there are many who feel that all our efforts should go to preventing war in the first place and that no war should be regarded as just. For such people the idea of conventions and moral principles within a war or revolution makes it all appear too much of a game, a game that once was tolerated but ought to be so no longer. Other Christian writers have looked at the matter somewhat differently. For them mankind always has been and, in the foreseeable future, always will be, in a state of actual or potential hostility. Outbreaks of violence are always likely. So, because war has so far been an incurable disease of mankind, it is better to acknowledge this and try to limit its effects. Life will go on after the fighting, and actions which would make the continuance of life impossible, such as the poisoning of wells, or the killing of children, must be forbidden.

So the first question to be asked of those who condemn terrorism in guerilla movements is, how do they react to nuclear weapons? Do they now support N.A.T.O. in which their threatened use plays such a vital part? On ethical questions there are many differences of opinion because of different basic beliefs. What we can ask of everyone who tries to think ethically is consistency. Our attitude to the prospect of direct attacks on civilians needs to be assessed *both* in relation to nuclear weapons *and* in relation to liberation movements.

Justifying non-combatant immunity

In a revolutionary war, or a war of any kind, is the object to kill the enemy? It has been argued that in Christian thinking in its early stages this was not the object. Rather the intention was to render the enemy harmless, to disable him, so that he could not inflict any further damage. It is true of course that very often enemy soldiers will be killed in action. But this is not the intention. The intention is to render them harmless and their deaths are an unintended side effect of this.

On this view of the matter the traditional immunity of non-combatants makes sense. Military actions have as their main purpose rendering the enemy harmless; they therefore concentrate on attacking soldiers and military installations. There is no need to attack civilians, unless they cease to be civilians by directly contributing to the war effort in some way. But though on this analysis the traditional immunity of non-combatants appears to be justified, in the modern world we come up against the claim that some ends are so essential that all means necessary to achieve them are justified. For example, some might argue that the preservation of western style democracy is crucial to the human spirit and that Russian communism is such a denial of all that makes human life worthwhile that any means necessary, even threatening to destroy millions of Russians, should be deployed to prevent communist expansion. It might also be argued that the liberation of a country from a colonial oppressor is so essential to the dignity and humanity of the colonised, that all means necessary to achieve that goal, including if need be the terrorism of civilians, might have to be used. The implications of this argument are frightening. So let's see if it will stand up to analysis.

There is a famous division of opinion amongst those who think about morality. The first group says that certain actions are intrinsically wrong, irrespective of the consequences; the second suggests that action can be judged right or wrong only in the light of the consequences. There are hard questions to be asked about both positions, but over against this second group it has been pointed out that morality is not just a matter of ends. The end and the means by which that end is to be attained are closely connected.

In a poem the idea that the writer is trying to communicate and the words that he chooses are really inseparable. The words are not just means to achieve an end, the communication of a particular idea: the feeling, the idea and the words form a unity. The same is true of morally right actions.

Suppose, for example, that we are trying to achieve a particular end, a society in which life and property are respected. In order for this to be achieved it is necessary that thieves are caught, that society is protected from them and that they be given a chance to change their ways. Let us suppose it is possible to threaten a particularly dangerous robber on the run by saying his child will be locked up and punished unless he gives himself up. Would this be justified? No, for punishing an innocent child would be a denial of the end which was being aimed at in the first place by trying to catch the thief. It would contradict the goal of a society in

which people were safe. With moral actions there is a fundamental unity between the action and the goal that action is
intended to bring about.

It cannot be denied that there are certain border-line cases.
For example, suppose that the criminal on the run had an
atomic device that he was capable of exploding and he was
threatening to do this in a large city. In that situation, if the
only way of getting through to the man, was to *threaten* to
hurt his child, it would have to be seriously considered. But it
is a mistake to judge everyday moral decision by extreme
situations which, like the one just mentioned, are mostly
hypothetical. In ordinary situations another important
consideration is paramount. If you threaten to hurt a child
with a view to getting his father to give himself up, you are
inflicting a known evil in order to obtain a problematic good.
The evil that is done is certainly done. The good that might
be obtained is only a possibility. It's a sound principle to avoid
doing what you know to be evil now when the good your are
seeking is uncertain.

Are liberation movements committed to terrorism?
From a moral point of view it matters what means are used in
a revolutionary war. Most people feel this. They also jump to
the conclusion that revolutionary armies are indiscriminate in
their fighting. A letter in *The Times* is a typical expression of
this point of view. 'Far from being "freedom fighters" these
men are blindly killing all those whose paths they cross . . . if
apartheid is morally indefensible, the indiscriminate
butchering of civilians is even more so.'

Here we come up against one of the major difficulties in
making a moral judgement in such matters—propaganda.
Each side in a dispute tends to spread stories of atrocities
committed by the other side. In Rhodesia much effort was
expended in telling people about the alleged horrors
committed by the Patriotic Front. On the other hand

organisations like the Catholic Institute for International Relations collected evidence of similar atrocities perpetrated by the government forces. It has even been suggested that some of these were done by the Rhodesian Selous Scouts dressed up as guerillas in order to discredit the enemy. It is always difficult to get at the truth of what has happened. Christians, amongst others, will certainly want to be aware of the powerful propaganda machines at work. And even when a particular fact is established beyond dispute, such as the civilian airliner shot down by the Patriotic Front, the matter may not be cut and dried. For the Patriotic Front claimed that a senior Army Commander was due to be travelling on the plane and it was he that they were trying to kill.

Some groups, such as the Provisional I.R.A., have always gone in for a high degree of indiscriminate terrorism. They have planted bombs in public places and claimed the deed as theirs even when scores of civilians have been killed. But not every armed group dedicated to the overthrow of a particular government has been so unselective and cruel. In Algeria, for example, where the war became bloody and bitter, terrorism was adopted by all sides. But for the Algerians it was not an easy decision. 'The decision to kill a civilian in the street is not an easy one, and no one comes to it lightly', wrote Franz Fanon. He then went on to detail the kind of people who were regarded as the legitimate object of attack, police superintendents with a reputation for torture, doctors who helped in the torturing or who administered truth drugs, those who reported patients to the authorities, and so on. This list reveals a fair degree of selectivity even in a war as cruel as the Algerian one.

The concern for human life is even more marked in the writings of Che Guevara, the South American revolutionary. This was expressed, first, in the strategy of keeping his guerilla band away from the centres of population so that they would not suffer reprisals. Second, he made a clear distinction between sabotage and terrorism. 'It is necessary to distinguish clearly between sabotage, a revolutionary and highly effective method of warfare, and terrorism, a measure that is generally ineffective and indiscriminate in its results, since it often makes victims of innocent people and destroys a large number of lives that would be valuable to the revolution.' He did, however, allow for exceptions, in the form of attacks on important or repressive enemies.

Che Guevara posed the question, 'Who are the combatants in guerilla warfare?', and answered it, 'On one side we have a group composed of the oppressor and his agents, the professional army . . . on the other side are the people of the nation or region involved.' But he knew that the soldiers in the government army were often illiterate peasants and he went out of the way to urge lenient treatment of prisoners. In battle he was particularly solicitous of the civilians in the area. Describing one battle he wrote, 'We were carefully instructed not to fire on the outlying buildings since they sheltered women and children, including the administrator's wife.' The account ended, 'The battle had lasted 2 hours 45 minutes and no civilian had been wounded despite the great number of shots that had been fired.'

Taken by itself Che Guevara's account does not give a balanced picture. First, it is his own account of what happened—others may see it differently. Second, what happened in Cuba is by no means representative of all guerilla struggles. We have only to remember the brutality and suffering in Vietnam, by both sides. The Vietcong for example had a policy of kidnapping or killing local officials, particularly village chiefs, and by 1963 13,000 of them had died as a result. But Che Guevara's account is important because it reminds us that guerilla warfare takes many forms. Not every campaign is like that of the Vietcong.

There is another factor even more significant. This is the one highlighted in Tabor's analysis, previously discussed, that guerilla warfare is primarily political and only secondarily military. On this theory the civilian population has a vital role to play. As Chairman Mao put it, 'With the common people of the whole country mobilised, we shall create a vast sea of humanity and drown the enemy in it'. On this principle it would clearly be self-defeating to alienate large sections of that civilian population by indiscriminate terrorism. The support of the civilian population is needed for the revolutionary struggle. And though of course the use of a certain amount of 'pressure' to persuade waverers to commit themselves to the revolutionary cause should not be overlooked, there is a clear limit to what this pressure can do without becoming counter-productive.

Tabor wrote, 'The population is the key to the entire struggle . . . it is the population that is doing the struggling. The guerilla who is of the people in a way which the government soldier cannot be fights with the support of the non-combatant civilian population . . . Without the consent and active aid of the people, the guerilla would be merely a bandit, and could not long survive.' The guerilla needs the civilian population on his side. There is then a powerful factor that will inhibit him from indulging in indiscriminate terrorism.

Examine the evidence: don't prejudge
The thesis argued in this chapter is that, from the moral point of view, the means used to carry out the fighting matter. Although any kind of war is brutal it is not true that 'anything goes'. In particular, the Christian tradition has always asserted that those not directly contributing to the war-effort should be immune from direct attack. This can be justified because the object of fighting is not to kill the enemy but to disable the aggressor. Killing harmless civilians does not help to do this. Further, from a philosophical point of view, the end we are trying to achieve and the means we are

using to obtain the end are closely bound up. At the least it is inconsistent to use means that contradict the desired end. If the aim is to bring about a society in which people are freed from cruelty and oppression it is a denial of that to try to attain such a society by cruel and oppressive means.

It is necessary to say to liberation movements, as it is necessary to say to governments, both those with and without nuclear weapons: direct attacks on harmless civilians are immoral.

It cannot be assumed, however, that liberation movements are by their nature committed to indiscriminate terrorism. From what the writings of Che Guevara reveal, and from what more general considerations about the whole nature of guerilla warfare confirm, liberation movements are likely to be more selective in their attacks than government propaganda machines allow. One of the major weapons of any governments experiencing a revolution is the propaganda picture of unprincipled terrorists ruthlessly killing everyone in their path. Sometimes, sadly, this has been true. At other times, though the war has been hard, and though there has been much suffering, attempts have been made to discriminate. As General Grivas said about the struggle against the British in Cyprus, 'The truth is that our form of war, in which a few hundred fell in four years, was more selective than most . . . we did not strike like bombers, at random. We shot only British servicemen who would have killed us if they could have fired the first shot, and civilians who were traitors or intelligence agents.'

In judging whether or not to support a guerilla movement a Christian should take account not only of the justice of the cause but of the means the group is using, or is going to use, to achieve its goals. But there is no need to assume that liberation movements are by their very nature committed to indiscriminate terrorism.

6
Postscript

But is it Christian?
A final question remains. Some people, broadly sympathetic
to the arguments put forward in this book, may find that a
niggling doubt lingers in the mind. Is there anything distinctively Christian about the approach to the question or about
the conclusion that has been reached? It almost seems that a
non-Christian might have argued in much the same kind of
way.

1. As we saw in chapter one, the desire to act in the most
loving way does not of itself tell us which course of action we
should pursue. Out of love one person will refuse to take up
arms and will trust that suffering, patiently borne, will in the
end win a victory for truth and justice. Another person, out
of love, will insist on taking up arms in order to stop powerless people being made to suffer at the hands of oppressors. If
the desire to act in the most loving way is regarded as something distinctively Christian then the latter course of action is
as Christian as the former.

2. There has been an attempt to approach the question in as
reasonable a way as possible. Being reasonable means trying to
see all sides of a question. A philosopher once remarked that
all ethics is a training in sympathy. One might have expected
a philosopher to stress other qualities. But it indicates that a
reasonable approach, far from being cold, as has sometimes
been pictured, is in fact rooted in the capacity to enter into
other people's situations. The reasonable person tries to look

at the question from the standpoint of everyone concerned, to weigh up all the factors. Earlier chapters stressed the importance of looking at potentially revolutionary situations both from the standpoint of those who have everything to lose and those who have everything to gain. It was emphasised that probable consequences have to be carefully weighed and the course of action least destructive to the majority chosen. This could be described as a reasonable approach. It could also be described as an attempt at sustained and systematic sympathy.

A reasonable approach also involves the attempt to liberate oneself from personal prejudice. This is of course the reverse side of trying to enter into the situations of other people. Unless we do this we simply reflect the views of our upbringing, social milieu, class or country. But to make the effort to transcened our own limited point of view is not only an attempt to think straight, it is an expression of Christian love.

A further feature of a reasonable approach is the attempt to be consistent. On many ethical questions there can be no final agreement because people make different assumptions and it is not usually possible, from a neutral point of view, to show that one set of assumptions is correct and the other false. But what we can ask of ourselves and other is consistency. If we accept that direct attacks on non-combatants are morally wrong then this judgement must be related both to obliteration bombing and to guerilla raids. Consistency sounds a dry idea, but it has a close connection with the Christian faith. God, we say, is faithful. We ourselves seek to be faithful in return. What is consistency but faithfulness in the realm of thought?

Reasonableness, far from being the enemy of Christian love, is in fact the expression of certain features of it.

3. It might be argued that the approach of this book was not distinctively Christian in the sense that it does not take a

clear biblical principle and make it supreme. A pacifist may feel that his position is distinctively Christian because it is based firmly on the teaching of Jesus. But did Jesus teach pacifism? Chapter one argued that he did not. Some people would point not so much to the teaching of Jesus as to his example on the cross; and they would refer to the epistles (especially 1 Peter) in which Christians are urged to bear suffering patiently. But there is a difference between suffering for your faith and suffering oppression as a human being. The former is something that all Christians might have to endure. There can be no question of taking up arms in defence of the faith. But when human beings are starved and exploited simply because they are poor and defenceless it is a very different matter.

There is obviously a difference also between an individual with no family or group responsibilities willingly undergoing suffering and someone who does have such responsibilities. If the father of a family chooses to put up with exploitation rather than retaliate he may be the cause of extra suffering for his family. When Luther said 'Suffering! Suffering! Cross! Cross! This and nothing else is the Christian Law', was he being fair to the rebellious peasants? They rose up not just on their own behalf but on behalf of their children. And though Luther was particularly angry that they championed social grievances in the name of Christianity it was in fact as citizens rather than Christians that they were suffering.

So although all Christians have to accept the possibility that they might have to suffer because they are believers and although in a particular situation of social oppression someone might choose to bear pain rather than join with those who have chosen to take up arms against the cause of it, this is not a way all Christians ought necessarily to take.

The fact is that Christian ethics is not just a matter of taking a single principle, even the hallowed one that we should bear suffering rather than inflict it on others, and applying it irrespective of other considerations. There are a number of principles that are fundamental to the Christian understanding of man and society and sometimes they conflict with one another. The principle of respect for life sometimes conflicts with the necessity of having an ordered or a just society, for example. The Christian just revolution tradition does not believe that only one principle is relevant. It deals with life in all its complexity and ambiguity and tries to provide a framework with which to think about the many difficult situations that arise when one group exploits and oppresses another. It does not believe that there are simple or simplistic solutions to problems that have many aspects to them. Nevertheless, there is in Christian thinking about war and revolution a recognisable tradition, and an accumulated wisdom, based upon and shaped by the Christian understanding of man and society.